A Mother-Father Complex

A Mother-Father Complex

ANDERS WENNERSTROM

Library of Congress Control Number:		2016920517
ISBN:	Softcover	978-1-5245-9673-6
	eBook	978-1-5245-9672-9

Print information available on the last page.

Rev. date: 01/16/2017

To order additional copies of this book, contact:
Xlibris
800-056-3182
www.Xlibrispublishing.co.uk
Orders@Xlibrispublishing.co.uk
753223

My thanks go to Sjöholms Public Accounting Firm in Karlshamn, Sweden that has helped me to publish this book.

If I Were Her

The dirt in your eyes:
I saw it,
and I shut my own eyes
for you not to see
how humiliated I felt,
because I didn't want
you to have that victory.

I felt the dirt in your eyes
on my skin,
and absorbed death
became my nature,
and so you died within me,
since you mirrored your
own hate
on my body.

The dirt in your eyes
was cleverly hidden
by a brain
that deconstructed
every judgement
that came to my mind.
And so I died within you,
because from point to point
in our conversations,
you moved me
as if I were a wife
from a planet
that I couldn't live on.

The dirt in your eyes
could have been good dirt
if you had allowed my love
to see the real you.
But you were only words
that moved and moved
and continued to move.
The little justice
I have always given you
could never be steady.
Instead, this justice
flew between walls,
with my insecurity
led by your scattered mind,
so that
I couldn't see
why you exist
for anything else
than for yourself.

My space
was always somebody else's
space,
and I felt not the belonging
where we were.
You gave other names to me
than what I am,
and I started to think
that others are me
without them loving me,
and that I can tell you,
you were those names
that should have given love
but instead gave me
a bankruptcy in my feelings
for you,
that, long nursed,
have been in need
not to see you
and not to live with you,
not to see
and not to live a life
with a person

I certainly
would have been in need
to feel love and affection for.
Because so is the world,
desire is the first principle
of real knowledge
however much dirt there is
inherently guiding the existence
of the knower,
and we need men who think,
and I would have needed your thoughts
many times, since we lost each other,
if you hadn't been a blank space
for me
that loved others
more than me.

You ate my face,
and you ate my tongue
alive.
You swallowed it,
squeezed already on my body.
My soul was somewhere
at the tapestries,
trying to move out of the apartment,
but then you took my legs
in your hands,
and you bent them aside
from each other,
with a calm and steady grip
over the situation.
As it was, I felt a joy
and even a great curiosity.
Then you said something,
"I love you,"
and my body started to feel
a need to pee,
so I peed on your stomach.

I felt your happiness
when you put your thing into me,
but your erected self
died soon after,
and I felt your desperation,
when you made
an excuse for yourself
for not doing better.
You excused yourself,
explaining you were high on drugs.
"Fucking drugs!
Fucking amateur lovemaker!
Don't you see?
Drugs are forbidden in the long run
when it comes to sex,
and you had been running
too long to stand up
for love
without escape."

ꝺ

I loved you.
I can assure you
that I loved you.
I loved you so much
that, completely
from free choice and
without pressure,
I porn-surfed in secret
when you were out of
the apartment,
because I wanted to learn
how to suck cock.
Before this, I had never seen porn,
and I had never sucked
someone's cock,
however much middle-aged
I am.
But now I learned
how to take care, with my teeth
not touching your glans,
but to use my lips, my mouth,
and my tongue like an open
hot spring.

Then I copied
the women porn stars,
and I did
what they are best at
to you.
I did this for you,
because I loved you so.
I was so happy to be with you.
When I was depressed,
my lovely mother, who loved you,
always said:
"Stay with Anders,
he will care for you."
It was exciting to be with you,
and you had always something
creative to say.
I remember I told you
that during my secret
porn-surfing, without your knowledge,
I had come across a legendary
male porn star who now is dead,
dead from AIDS,
John Holmes,

and I described for you
his incredible dick,
so huge,
and I said it felt, yes, it felt
almost ridiculous,
and you said,
"The magnitude of John Holmes
doesn't exist in today's society
without perversion."
"And John wasn't," you said, "a perverse person
or doing any perverse things
but just being a love-maker
for the sake of sexual freedom."
"There isn't a place for such men anymore,"
you said.
You were able to give information
and even be witty at the same time.
I was very impressed by your knowledge
when you said that the male
sexual organ has lessened in size
over a historical period
and that we really don't know
where it will end.

I even remember how
I gave you the lion's kiss
and the mouse's kiss,
and as I now understand,
you stayed with me
for another month
because of the mouse's kiss.
The mouse's kiss is like tickling
a little space on your face
with minimal movements
of your tongue.
I felt we were both small and cute,
socially in life,
as I felt our communion
as a space of indigenous love,
not for others to look at.
We had our secrets,
and I even cuddled
with your two little teddy bears
that you liked to hold in your hands
when you slept.
Yes, I know,

I even bought one
of them for you,
after your
beloved little pink pig,
which your mother
had given you before
you got to Dublin,
disappeared from
your rented room.
And yes, I know, I was even a bit jealous
of your teddy bears.
Sometimes, I felt they meant
more to you than I did.
However, I didn't really understand
your situation in society,
as I do today.
You talked a lot
about influence,
but I didn't really understand
your perception of that.
Today, I know you were

in a melting pot
of other people's thoughts,
and it might be that I can
forgive the one
who suddenly and without great notice
left me, blind to the deep connection
we had.
This man you were,
who made me so happy
that I did things
that never would have come
to mind without you,
who said good bye
in just a second,
opened the door
and disappeared from me
like a shadow
in some kind of a spy movie,
when a friend suddenly
becomes the worst enemy in my life.

My Dog Father Shadow and My Pussycat Mother Tongue

𝒯

Old man sits on a chair,
and his dog dies from a bullet
from a terrorist.

The dog has an open scar,
dead for no reason at all.

Then the dog starts to walk again,
and it only stops at its master's
leg, sniffing the Manchester cotton,
breathing in the old man's smell.

Then the terrorist understood;
he is a grandson of the old man,
and he shot the old man's dog
with a stone,
a stone he found on the street
and just randomly picked up
and used because he had, until then,
not understood that he is his grandfather's
heir.

The old man forgave
but wasn't happy until
the dog had forgiven,
a forgiving that the dog gave
when the grandson
didn't do the negatively randomly anymore,
or didn't do the negatively routine,
because he is a boy.

The grandson and the dog
became friends
because they really only had each other;
after that, the grandfather
became blind.

Grandfather's blindness
made him fall on stairs
and on the pavement.
One day, he died,
over three hundred years old,
and the last thing he said
was that "revolutions are a good thing,
as long as they don't cut your head off."

The dog started to bark
and yell
but looked with love on the grandson.
They then ate a meal
with potato from the region
and beef that the dog
had mixed up with eggs, milk, water,
some flour, salt, and onion.

ℰ

My pussycat mother tongue
gave a command,
and I said no.
She gave me another command,
and I still said no.

"Follow me,"
my pussycat mother tongue said,
and I said no.

"Follow me down the basement
and help me with the cleaning,"
my pussycat mother tongue said to me,
and I said no.

"You know what we call somebody
like you?" my mother tongue pussycat asked.
"A toddler, or in Swedish,
du är en unge inte torr bakom öronen.
You know what that means in English?
It means you are a toddler,
not dry behind your ears."

I couldn't say then,
but I say it now:
I have anxieties
(my mother tongue pussycat),
and sometimes I can't move myself
out of bed.
I just can't, and I have a dim light
in front of my eyes,
where I hear my mother tongue pussycat
telling me I can't.

So I ask myself:
Should I do as you say,
or as you intentionally say?

And suddenly you said,
"I will follow you,
and I will follow you
until I know how we
can be friends."

And I said,
"I will walk,
and I will walk
until I know who you are."

✦

"I gave you a million
for Africa's sake,
when you were born,"
my dog says
in my dreams.
"And I gave you
your mother
as a diamond
to hang around your neck,"
he whispered,
when I woke up.
"I even gave you
my friends
as a testicle
to hold in your hands
when the wind blows
at its most serious level,"
he continued.

I know,
I say to myself,
in a lonely apartment.
And you know what,
my dog shadow father?
I was at a café, and
I gave the girl who served me
my satisfaction,
and she sent
a thousand Swedish krona
right into my ears
because I was friendly.
She did it with your money,
of course,
but she acted it out,
even though
it was your money
that paid her
to make me believe
that life isn't a shitty bastard
place to be at,
and that is good
and something new to me.

But the fact is,
I lost a million
already when
I started to communicate
with friends at my age,
early in life.
They told me
I was ugly,
and then
my life was over,
and your million
was for no use
at all.

And my mother had costed
me a journey
that might have costed me
every jewel
you have hung around my neck.
Your own friends you gave me
have been my raw models,
but when the wind blew
at its most serious level,
they dissolved
as if they were blown bubbles.

It's not the end of the story,
but once I was in England,
sick, humiliated, and lost,
and you were in Sweden
when you started to count my age
in my mind.
You said:
Now you are three years old;
and now you are twenty;
and now you are eighty-eight;
and now you are in childhood again,
being two.
You are in England doing a master's,
and you are right now
two years old.
Would it not be in time
to believe what I believe in?

What is that?

I asked my mother tongue pussycat.

"That is work," she said,

"and only for that question are you

twenty-five, as you should be."

But I feel questioned all the time,

I said.

"You hesitate, and you are only four years old

right now,"

my pussycat mother tongue prolonged.

"I feel that nobody likes me.

I actually feel hated,"

I said.

"And now your actual age is thirteen,"

she continued.

Okay, I get your point,

I shouldn't argue like that.
"And now you are a grown-up,
being sixty years old,
like your father.
Stay there, if you can," she said.
But my father isn't able,
I quarreled.
"Alright," my pussycat mother tongue said,
"now you are only one year old
and you are still doing a master's in England,
a master's you won't have success with.
However, I have hope for you.
It's just that the time isn't right at the moment.
You need to live a hundred more years
before the manufacturer
can take your point of view."

&

"Write," says my dog father shadow.
Yes, I will, I say,
and I go to the computer,
and I write,
trying to understand myself.
"I'll give you hundred Swedish krona
for every idea
you let into your head
and send out to other people,"
my dog father shadow says to me.

However, I need food, I say,
but I am anxious to go out
and get me a meal.
"I'll give you ten dollars
in pleasure
if you go out and spend
some money
on a tasteful meal,"
my dog father shadow points out.
And I do: I go out,
and I spend money
on a meal,
and there we go.
I survived it.
It was even a good experience,
I have to remark.

But yesterday night
I drank so terribly much
that I will die
in the upcoming
workweek.
I think I overdid it this time,
I said in an insecure
mind of regrets.

"Each minute with hangover regrets,
I will pay you through and through,
until you believe,
until you believe,
that it's not a crime,
that it's not
a crime, to take some pain
for the sake of fun,"
my dog father shadow
whispers smoothly in my head.
"And it's not a crime
to celebrate yourself,
even if you are alone
in this world,"
he continues.

I feel better right now,
I claim as my bitterness
is losing its grip
over my situation,
speaking with my dog father shadow.
"Write again,"
my dog father shadow says.
And I write:
I write the negative,
and I write the positive.
But sometimes I get anxiety
for the things I wrote,
and then I go to bed,
mumbling within myself,
wondering if I am completely stupid;
who provokes the world as I do?

"Resist,"
I hear my dog father shadow say,
as he touches me right
where it hurts,
right on my soul,
so that I can't escape the pain.
But as I stay there,
right on the spot where it hurts,
even as it moves
and I follow it,
I start to feel a joyful feeling,
and it smiles at me,
telling me with the dog's voice
that even if people aren't agreeing
with you,
you will make friends,
only if you stay up
for your words.

"And the only rule I give you,"
my dog father shadow claims,
"is to not hate
the people who don't
agree with you,
and you will get
pleasure
from something
for its own sake."

"So write," my dog father shadow says,
"because we need to learn
that our thoughts
aren't a heritage
but a communion
(do you see the point here?
It's not an ownership of things
but a common feeling together),
in its own sake,
a communion
that shares
the negative with the positive,
and you know that.
That's why I ask you to write,"
he says.

"You learned early in life
to take pain from other people's pain,
also my pain," he says,
"and right now
are your pen
the pain you grew up with,
and it is the only magical thing
you can trust,"
my dog father shadow whispers softly.

It's hurtful sometimes,
to think, sir, I say,
but I am happy I can write
for you, my dog father shadow.
I gesture with my hands,
not regretting any
of the negations
I have done to my discourse.

♂

"Yes, write,"
my pussycat mother tongue
tells me,
"because then you can see
my negations of you
as a resource
you never thought
could be of any use.
So please write my words
as if I were
the concrete form
of your ideas,
a cat among other cats
that think otherwise
than what people think
they think.
And, please, let this
pussycat have fun
so that I don't
always need to feel that life
is just another name
for insolvent hardship."

♀

Printed in the United States
By Bookmasters